CW00661695

MARCUS IS
WALKING

BY
JOAN ACKERMANN

★

★

DRAMATISTS
PLAY SERVICE
INC.

MARCUS IS WALKING
Copyright © 1999, Joan Ackermann

All Rights Reserved

SPECIAL NOTE
Anyone receiving permission to produce MARCUS IS WALKING is required to give credit to the Author as sole and exclusive Author of the Play on the title page of all programs distributed in connection with performances of the Play and in all instances in which the title of the Play appears for purposes of advertising, publicizing or otherwise exploiting the Play and/or a production thereof. The name of the Author must appear on a separate line, in which no other name appears, immediately beneath the title and in size of type equal to 50% of the size of the largest, most prominent letter used for the title of the Play. No person, firm or entity may receive credit larger or more prominent than that accorded the Author. The following acknowledgment must appear on the title page in all programs distributed in connection with performances of the Play:

Originally commissioned and produced by Otterbein College,
May 1997, Westerville, OH. Director: Christina Kirk;
Artistic Director: Dennis Romer; Chairperson: John Stefano.

SPECIAL NOTE ON SONGS AND RECORDINGS
For performances of copyrighted songs, arrangements or recordings mentioned in this Play, the permission of the copyright owner(s) must be obtained. Other songs, arrangements or recordings may be substituted provided permission from the copyright owner(s) of such songs, arrangements or recordings is obtained; or songs, arrangements or recordings in the public domain may be substituted.

For my brother Rick,
Kathryn, and Jane

with love ...

MARCUS IS WALKING was commissioned by and first performed at Otterbein College in Westerville, Ohio, in May, 1997. It was directed by Christina Kirk. The cast was as follows:

ELLEN, SUZIE, THE LEMON
LISA, GREAT GRANNIE .... Amber Mellott
MICHAEL, RICK, HENRY
JEAN-LUC .... Ben Hauck
MALE DANCER, STANLEY,
DEAN, GERALD .... Michael Faber
HEIDIE, CAITLIN, THE WITCH
FEMALE DANCER, RUTHIE .... Kathryn Felsenthal
JAY, MARCUS, QUEENIE
ANNE .... Nikki Hersh
ZACK, MARTY, PHILIP
TERRENCE .... Nathan Weaver

MARCUS IS WALKING was produced by Mixed Company Theatre in Great Barrington, Massachusetts, in August, 1997. It was directed by Robert Russell. The cast was as follows:

MICHAEL, ZACK, HENRY
JEAN-LUC .... Jeffrey Albani, Michael Marlowe
ELLEN, SUZIE, LISA
GREAT GRANNIE .... Karyn Lee
DMITRY, RICK, PHILIP
MARTY, GERALD .... Rick Pepper
JAY, QUEENIE, RUTHIE
THE WITCH .... Francine Ciccarelli, Barbara Cardillo
HEIDIE, CAITLIN, ANNE
THE LEMON .... Anne Undeland
GABE, DEAN, TERRENCE .... Gabe Patel
MARCUS .... Joan Ackermann

ACKNOWLEDGMENTS

Thank you Dana White, Christina Kirk, and the gifted students at Otterbein College who first brought this play to life.

PLAYWRIGHT'S NOTE: Otterbein College commissioned this play which had been kicking around in my head for a while. It's the hundredth anniversary of cars and time, I think, to ponder their presence in our lives and our presence in theirs. Although their function is to take us from one place to another, we are, in fact, in a place when we are in them. A place with its own specific emotions, behavior, familiarity. We sit, we look straight ahead, we move. Our minds go on journeys of their own. Alone, we become more alone; with others, our togetherness becomes more pronounced. I'm indebted to A.R. Gurney whose wonderful play *The Dining Room* helped in part to inspire the format of this play. Given the quick scene changes and number of characters, it's important that the characters not be reduced to caricature. I hope you and your audiences have a scenic, highly satisfying road trip. Good luck.

J.A.

SET

The simplest possible car. Two car seats (van seats work well) mounted on carpeted platforms; the back seat a foot higher than the front. A steering wheel on a steering column. No more than that is needed. The car is the central character of the play and needs to hold center stage.

CAST

Three men, three women. Each actor plays four or five parts — a variety of ages and characters.

SOUND

Lots of good road tunes. In our production at Mixed Company we kicked back into the same bluegrass piece between all scenes in the first act to keep it moving.

MARCUS IS WALKING

ACT ONE

Scene 1

Michael and Ellen, in their late twenties/early thirties, are equally anxious. Michael — dressed in corduroy trousers, worn button-down Oxford shirt and tie — is driving too fast, leaning forward, holding the steering wheel tightly. Ellen, dressed up nicely in skirt and sweater, clutches the armrest, very nervous about his driving.

ELLEN. We're not lost.

MICHAEL. *(Thinks they're lost.)* No.

ELLEN. We're not.

MICHAEL. Great. *(Pause.)*

ELLEN. Could you please slow down? *(He doesn't. She grips her seat.)* Michael, it's seven twenty-eight. We're not late yet.

MICHAEL. What are we looking for?

ELLEN. A rotary. They're having cocktails first and then dinner. We're not late.

MICHAEL. We're not late, we're not lost, we're on the wrong road.

ELLEN. We're not on the wrong road.

MICHAEL. We're on the wrong road.

ELLEN. We're not on the wrong road.

MICHAEL. What's the name of the road?

ELLEN. What road?

MICHAEL. The road we're supposed to be on. *(Pause.)* Well?

ELLEN. I don't know.

MICHAEL. Ellen, *you* got the directions. You're supposed to know what road we're supposed to be on. *(Pause.)*
ELLEN. What road are we on?
MICHAEL. We're on Route 6 east.
ELLEN. That's the road. *(He glances at her.)* We're supposed to be on. If you don't believe me, stop and ask that man.
MICHAEL. Ask him what?
ELLEN. If this road goes to a rotary.
MICHAEL. No.
ELLEN. Why not? *(Michael turns the wheel suddenly. Lurching.)* Michael, you're going to spill the soup.
MICHAEL. What soup?
ELLEN. The soup in the back.
MICHAEL. There's soup in the back?
ELLEN. I made soup. It's a potluck.
MICHAEL. What's a potluck?
ELLEN. The dinner we're going to. Is potluck. Everybody brings something to eat. A dish.
MICHAEL. *(His tension mounting.)* That's *insane*. What if everybody brings the same thing?
ELLEN. They don't. Michael, lighten up.
MICHAEL. What kind of soup?
ELLEN. Pea.
MICHAEL. Pea soup?
ELLEN. Yes, pea soup. *(Pause.)*
MICHAEL. They know you're bringing pea soup?
ELLEN. I told Pauline I'd bring pea soup.
MICHAEL. Who's Pauline?
ELLEN. Pauline is the wife of the head of the English Department. The man who hired you. The man whose house we're going to.
MICHAEL. Or not. *(Pause.)* Did she ask you to bring soup, any kind of soup, or specifically pea soup?
ELLEN. She asked me what I wanted to bring and I said soup.
MICHAEL. So she doesn't know it's pea.
ELLEN. No. *(Pause.)*
MICHAEL. It seems a little ...
ELLEN. What?

MICHAEL. Well. Mundane.

ELLEN. It's not mundane. It's delicious. It's full of herbs. *Herbes de Provence.*

MICHAEL. Ellen, this is a very … high-powered department. These guys are into hermeneutics. Deconstruction.

ELLEN. Michael, *please* slow down.

MICHAEL. This is the wrong road.

ELLEN. Well, you're going to end up farther down the wrong road faster.

MICHAEL. I'm turning around.

ELLEN. Fine. Be late. *(He pulls over, stopping the car and letting it idle.)*

MICHAEL. Let me see the directions.

ELLEN. You won't be able to read them.

MICHAEL. Let me see them. *(Reluctantly, she hands him an envelope with sketches on it.)* I can't read a word of this. *(Pointing.)* What is this?

ELLEN. It's the sycamore tree. We turned at.

MICHAEL. This says sycamore tree?

ELLEN. It doesn't say sycamore tree. It *is* a sycamore tree. *(He stares at her. Studies the drawing.)*

MICHAEL. What is this?

ELLEN. Michael, I don't like your tone.

MICHAEL. Ellen, this party is for me. This dinner party is for me, this potluck event is an opportunity for the whole department to meet me and I'm not there and they are.

ELLEN. No, they're not, they're not all there yet.

MICHAEL. What does this say?

ELLEN. That's the blue-grey house we turned left at. Those are columns. On the front porch.

MICHAEL. Why can't you write down directions in English.

ELLEN. They're symbols, Michael. Symbolism.

MICHAEL. We turned here? At this house?

ELLEN. Yes, we turned left there.

MICHAEL. And then what did we do?

ELLEN. We turned right at the fire station.

MICHAEL. *(Trying.)* Fire station?

ELLEN. On the right side of the page means turn right, on the left, left.

MICHAEL. I can't … *(Highly frustrated.)* Where is north? Ellen?

ELLEN. Huh?

MICHAEL. Where is north?

ELLEN. You're being obnoxious. North on the envelope or north out there?

MICHAEL. North on the envelope. I know where north out there is.

ELLEN. I don't know. *(He hands her back the envelope. Puts his face in his hands.)*

MICHAEL. I'm gonna lose my job. My reputation is already shit before I even start. *(Ellen watches someone walking by.)*

ELLEN. Let's ask her.

MICHAEL. Who?

ELLEN. Her.

MICHAEL. Her? That *woman? (As if Ellen's insane.)* Ask her what?

ELLEN. If there's a rotary up ahead.

MICHAEL. No! No! Don't ask her anything. *(She rolls down the window. He abruptly pulls back onto the road.)*

ELLEN. Excuse me! Hi, excuse me, is there a rotary up along this road? *(They speed away. Ellen leans back in.)* Why do men never ask for directions? Why don't they? What is it? Why are you incapable of asking a friendly stranger a friendly reasonable question that that person has had themselves many times?

MICHAEL. That's horrific grammar.

ELLEN. What do you have to hide? You can't admit for one second of one day you're just a little bit unclear, a little bit hazy about your whereabouts, what is so terribly embarrassing about that? You'd ask somebody what time it is, why can't you ask them where a particular geographic location is, it's not like we're in a war zone, you're divulging the whereabouts of your troops, Michael if you don't slow down, I'm going to leave you. I swear, I am not going to be married to someone who drives like a maniac and is insensitive to my feelings.

MICHAEL. *(In a panic.)* If I can't make it to dinner on time, how am I going to make it to class on time, that's what they're wondering. That's what they're saying right now to each other over their pots and their luck. Jesus Christ, you never wanted me to

12

take this job. You didn't want to move here. You didn't want to leave New York. That's why you didn't write down the directions intelligibly. That's why you made pea soup!

ELLEN. God, I *hate* the way you drive!!

MICHAEL. I *hate* the way you ride!!

ELLEN. I would ride better if you would drive better!!

MICHAEL. I would drive better if you were capable of writing down directions!! *(Silence. Tension.)*

ELLEN. *(Thrilled.)* There it is!

MICHAEL. What?

ELLEN. The rotary. Take a right, here. Quick, now.

MICHAEL. Edmund Street? *(He takes a right.)*

ELLEN. Second driveway.

MICHAEL. He lives on Edmund Street?

ELLEN. Right here. This driveway here. Wisteria on the mailbox.

MICHAEL. 103? Is that what she told you, 103?

ELLEN. Park by the dumpster.

MICHAEL. Why do they have a dumpster? You're sure this is the right house?

ELLEN. They're putting on a new roof.

MICHAEL. A new roof?

ELLEN. It's constructive deconstruction.

MICHAEL. Oh my God, there's Rafferty, I can see him through the window. Oh … God …

ELLEN. See? They're still having drinks. We're not late. *(Lovingly.)* Take a deep breath.

MICHAEL. Okay. *(Takes a quick shallow breath.)* Okay. *(He turns off the motor. They both get out of the car. He puts on an old worn tweed jacket he grabs out of the back window while she opens the back door and gets the soup.)* How do I look?

ELLEN. You look great.

MICHAEL. I look okay?

ELLEN. Yup. Professorial.

MICHAEL. You have the soup?

ELLEN. I have the soup. *(He comes around and kisses her quickly on the lips, looking at Rafferty in the window. Moves ahead. Stops. Turns, looks at her. Takes a breath, really taking her in. Moves back to her and gives her a meaningful kiss. Takes the soup from her and starts to go.)* Michael? *(He looks back at her.)* Which way is north?

MICHAEL. *(Pointing.)* That way. *(She looks that way as he goes ahead.)*

ELLEN. Hunh. *(Impressed, to herself.)* Pretty good. *(She follows him.)*

Scene 2

A dance. The actor need not be a dancer; he just needs to move freely, inspired and excited about his date. A man dressed up in a white tuxedo drives, beaming with delight, a bouquet of red roses in the passenger seat. He grooms himself in the rear-view mirror, stroking back his hair, admiring himself. Smiling, he turns to the bouquet, whispers sweet nothings to it. He mimes reaching for a cassette and puts it in, something like Tony Bennet's "Stepping Out."* The dance begins. Moving to the music, he stops the car, presses a button and assists the convertible roof back. He jumps jauntily out of the car and dances around in uninhibited movements, possibly reaching for the roses as his dancing partner, possibly tripping, gleefully waving at passers-by. He is madly in love, fueled by the romantic prospects of the night ahead. The more unrestrained and exuberant his movements, the more engaging and endearing the dance will be. Near the end, he leaps back into the car, closes the door, smiles at himself in the mirror, and starts the car up again as the music ends. Whatever the choreography, dancer should enjoy himself.

---

* See Special Note on Songs and Recordings on copyright page.

Scene 3

It is dusk. Two seventeen-year-old girls in Catholic School uniforms — jumpers or skirt and white blouses — are standing behind the car, looking down. Jay, the leader of the group, serious, an intellectual, wears a beret and black Converse sneakers. Heidie, more demure and a follower, wears matching knee socks and penny loafers. Suzie, fifteen, also in uniform, sits in the back seat. She has an overflowing four-subject notebook on her lap in which she writes with a fat pink pen. She holds up and reads the Cliff Notes, *or another study guide, for* Moby Dick.

JAY. *(Groaning.)* Oh no …

HEIDIE. Well. I guess you did.

JAY. Shit!

HEIDIE. I didn't think you did. I didn't feel anything.

JAY. I did. *He* did.

HEIDIE. I don't think he felt anything, Jay, I really don't. I don't think he had time. I think before his nerve cells could get to his brain, his brain was already squished. Jay, don't feel bad.

SUZIE. *(Disgusted.)* These are the most poorly written Cliff Notes I have ever read.

HEIDIE. *(Trying to console her.)* He didn't suffer. He didn't feel any pain. *(Jay collapses on the road; sits, cross-legged, head in hands.)*

SUZIE. I wasted four hours of my life reading them, I've gotten nothing out of them, nothing, zero. I could have spared myself and read the friggin' book.

HEIDIE. Jay …

SUZIE. Jay, you've *got* to help me. I have three papers due Monday, my average in English so far this term is 43. Mr. Scrotumface told me today.

HEIDIE. Look, Jay, he's totally flat. He died in a heartbeat, like so fast, like faster than he could swallow than he could *think* about

15

swallowing. I'm not kidding, by the time the tire got to the front end of him …

JAY. *(Interrupting.)* Heidie. He died fast, but he's dead forever.

SUZIE. Geez, you guys, it's just a chipmunk, get over it. Jay, what is the symbol, *please?* Is it Ahab's peg-leg, is it the whale? Is it a good symbol? Is it a bad symbol?

HEIDIE. It's not your fault. You didn't kill him. *(With her head down, Jay shakes her head.)*

SUZIE. Frankly, I think a wooden leg and an albino whale are both pretty *pathetic* symbols. Moby Dickhead, the only reason this book is a classic is 'cause it's old.

JAY. I killed him. *(Jay gets up and moves away. Heidie follows her.)*

SUZIE. *(Reading from her study guide.)* "Captain Ahab's obsessive pursuit of the great white whale resonates in a dual plane of tranquility and good, as well as terror and evil." Oh that's very clear, that is crystal clear, that is Ph.D. thinking. Who wrote this drek, he can't even make up his mind.

HEIDIE. He couldn't make up his mind. You weren't driving recklessly, it's not like you were going ninety, you were only going like maybe like thirty, like maybe thirty-five. You tried to miss him. He was going back and forth, back and forth. He was totally indecisive.

SUZIE. *(Reading from the front.)* Some bozo at the University of Nebraska. Some loser academic trying to get tenure, get published.

HEIDIE. You want to bury it? Him?

JAY. *(Forlorn.)* I don't know. *(Suzie starts writing in her notebook.)*

SUZIE. Take him to school. They'll serve him for lunch, roadkill sandwich that's about what they serve anyway, those Sloppy Joes.

HEIDIE. *(Sharply.)* Suzie. Just cut it. You want to light a candle? I have a candle in my pack. Jay?

JAY. No. Thanks.

SUZIE. Frankly, I think the world could get along very well without symbolism.

HEIDIE. He has two lines on his back. Like the lines of a highway.

SUZIE. Symbolism just means you can't express yourself clearly well in the first place.

JAY. God, I feel so bad.

SUZIE. Hey, those are the risks of country living.

JAY. Those aren't the risks of country living. This animal didn't

16

make a conscious choice to live in the country and accept its risks. This isn't even the country to him, it's just the planet.

SUZIE. I meant *you, duh*. From a human perspective, the risks of country living are that every now and then you kill some wildlife. You become a murderer.

HEIDIE. She is not a murderer. *(To Jay.)* Have you ever run over anything before?

JAY. Never.

HEIDIE. I don't think I have.

SUZIE. You probably have. You probably have and you didn't know it. You've probably slaughtered thousands of bugs and insects and frogs and mitochondria.

HEIDIE. Suzie, shut up.

SUZIE. How's this? *(Reading from her notebook.)* "The relationship between Captain Ahab, the man, and Moby Dick, the whale, is very interesting and awesomely intense." *(Counting.)* Eighteen words. Only nine hundred and eighty-something to go.

JAY. I feel like we should eat him.

HEIDIE. Eat him? You really do? Jay? *(Jay is studying him.)*

JAY. Yeah. Bless him and ingest him. Take his spirit into ours. Give his death some purpose.

SUZIE. I can just see at McDonald's. Chipmunk McNuggets.

HIEDIE. I wonder where he was going.

SUZIE. Speaking of going, the video store's gonna close, you guys.

JAY. You go. I'm not going.

HEIDIE. What?

JAY. I'm not going to drive. Ever again.

HEIDIE. Jay …

JAY. I'm gonna walk home. I'll meet you back there.

SUZIE. Don't you think you're being a little *radical?*

HEIDIE. That's like five miles.

JAY. I'm not gonna walk on the road. I'm gonna walk through the woods.

HEIDIE. Jay …

JAY. Roads are just killing fields. Killing fields for innocent animals who are walking innocently along, one mile an hour, a normal God-given speed. The speed they were meant to travel.

HEIDIE. I can't drive a stick shift and Suzie can't drive at all.

17

SUZIE. Excuse me, I'm not old enough.

JAY. Well. I'm sorry, I'm not driving. I'm not getting back in that car.

SUZIE. I tell you one thing. I am not walking five miles. No way.

HEIDIE. You're gonna leave your parents' car here?

JAY. Yeah. *(Jay leans over.)*

HEIDIE. What are you doing?

JAY. I'm going to take him home and bury him.

SUZIE. Don't you think you are being just slightly *fanatic?*

HEIDIE. You're picking him up with your bare hands?

SUZIE. Oh *gross.*

HEIDIE. I don't think you should touch him.

JAY. I killed him. The least I can do is touch him. *(Holding the chipmunk in her hands, Jay starts to leave.)* Bye.

HEIDIE. You're really gonna walk through the woods?

JAY. Heidie. For centuries human beings walked through the woods. Lived in the woods. There were no roads, no massive black ugly scars on the planet.

HEIDIE. It's gonna be dark pretty soon.

JAY. Not as dark as it is inside this little guy's head.

SUZIE. This is sick. This is demented. Jay, is the symbol the leg or the whale and is it bad or good just quick *please* tell me.

JAY. The symbol is the car. And it's very, very bad. *(Jay exits.)*

HEIDIE. Jay …

SUZIE. Oh, Jesus, I'm screwed. I am screwed. *(Pause.)*

HEIDIE. I'm going with her.

SUZIE. What?

HEIDIE. I'm going with her.

SUZIE. You're kidding.

HEIDIE. No. *(Heidie opens the passenger door and gets out her jacket, which she puts on, does up, and her backpack.)*

SUZIE. OhmyGod, this is getting out of hand. Wait a minute. Just, please, what is going on. We were going out for a video, we were gonna get some pizza, what is this? Heidie, for heaven's sake, don't go.

HEIDIE. I have to. I don't want her walking through the woods by herself. Just stay in the car. Her dad will be by soon.

SUZIE. Yeah, what if some weird psycho-killer comes first?

HEIDIE. You'll be fine.

SUZIE. *Fine* slashed in *pieces.*
HEIDIE. Jay! Jay, wait! *(Heidie exits.)*
SUZIE. *People.* Get *real!* (Suzie is alone. After ten lonesome fearful seconds, she jumps out of the car and screams at the top of her voice.) Don't leave me alone! Don't leave me ALONE! You're not supposed to leave me alone, you're supposed to take care of me! My mother trusted you to take care of me. COME BACK!! It's not my fault you killed a chipmunk! It's not my fault! I didn't run under the car and run back and forth and make the wrong decision and get nailed! I didn't make this car, I didn't make this road, I'm not responsible for modern civilization! You guys! I know I'm obnoxious, I know nobody can stand me, but you're supposed to take care of me!! Come back!! (She suddenly hears a car approaching. She looks up the road toward the approaching headlights. Gets scared; ducks down. Can't decide whether to wave the car down or hide. Gets up; runs behind the car out onto the road to wave it down. Changes her mind. Runs back and ducks down. Repeats this movement several times, running back and forth behind the car. Her movements should imitate the chipmunk's before he was hit. Finally she decides to hide from the car, which passes. Heidie and Jay enter. Jay gets in the driver's seat and Heidie gets in the passenger seat. Greatly shaken, Suzie just stares at them.)
HEIDIE. Get in the car, Suzie. (Suzie gets in the back seat. Jay starts up the car, starts driving.)
SUZIE. Why did you come back?
HEIDIE. 'Cause you were hysterical. *(Silence.)*
SUZIE. Where's the chipmunk?
JAY. In my pocket.
SUZIE. I'll hold him for you. *(Heidie looks back at Suzie. Lights fade.)*

Scene 4

Gabe, an actor, is driving to the theatre, intensely practicing his lines for Hamlet for an opening that night. He is a good actor but anxious about getting reviewed. A box with a slice of pizza in it is on the passenger seat.

GABE.   Now I am alone.
O, what a rogue and pleasant slave am I!
Is it not monstrous that this player here,
But in a fiction, in a dream of passion,
Could force his soul so to his own conceit
That from her working all his visage waned,
Tears in his eyes, distraction in his aspect,
A broken voice, and his whole function suiting
With forms to his conceit? And all for nothing,
For Hecuba!
(He looks in his side window, sticks out his arm, waving on a car.)
Go, go, *go*. Get thee, get thee, *get thee. (Sinks back into character.)*
What's Hecuba to him, or he to Hecuba,
That he should weep for her? What would he do
Had he the motive and the cue for passion
That I have? He would drown the stage with tears
And cleave the general ear with horrid speech
Get off my ass, buddy. *(Looking in the rearview mirror.)* Get off
my ass.
Make mad the guilty and appall the free,
Confound the ignorant, and amaze indeed
The very faculties of eyes and ears.
(Looks, annoyed, again in rearview mirror.)
Yet I,
A dull and muddy-mettled rascal, peak
Like John-a-dreams, unpregnant of my cause,
And can say nothing.

(He holds up his middle finger to guy behind. Tries to remember where he is in his soliloquy.)

And can say nothing ...
And can say nothing ...

Shit.

Now I am alone ...
Soon I will be on stage ...
Soon I will be on stage ... getting reviewed ...
No, not for a king,
Upon whose property and most dear life
A damned defeat was made. Am I a coward?
Who calls me villain? Breaks my pate across?
Plucks off my beard and blows it in my face?

Drives up my fucking *ass?*

Tweaks me by the nose? Who does this me?

Pass me, just fucking pass me ... *(His anger feeds his performance.)*

Ha, 'swounds, I should take it, for it cannot be
But I am pigeon-livered and lack gall
To make oppression bitter, or ere this
I should ha' fatted all the region kites
With this slave's offal.

(He suddenly steps on the brake. There is the sound of a loud CAR CRASH. Gabe smiles, chuckles. Leaps out. Turns around. His performance is magnificent.)

Bloody, bawdy villain!

Remorseless, treacherous, lecherous, kindless villain!

(Dmitry, the Czech cab driver, storms on; stunned, enraged, disbelieving. He looks behind the car at his imaginary smashed cab.)

O, vengeance!

DMITRY.   You *crazy?* You crazy your *mind?* You're *thinking??* *What? What??!*

GABE.   Vengeance!

DMITRY.   You *stop?* Like this, you *stop?* My *cab.* My *taxicar. Look,* is *bang!!* Fuckshit. Fuckshit.

GABE.   This is most brave,
That I, the son of a dear father murdered
Prompted to my revenge by heaven and hell
Must like a whore unpack my heart with words

21

And fall a-cursing like a very drab,
A scullion!
(Dmitry comes at him, rolling up his sleeves.)
DMITRY. Fuckshit. I gonna fuckshit you. *(Dmitry makes a fist, moves toward Gabe and starts throwing punches at him. Gabe reaches into the back seat of his car and elegantly and nimbly pulls out a foil, which he aims at Dmitry.)*
GABE.   Fie upon't. Foh! Fie upon't!
(Gabe makes a dramatic gesture with the sword at Dmitry who takes off his cap, steps back, afraid. With a deft handling of the sword, Gabe moves him backwards, speaking intently, pointedly, mesmorizingly.)

　　　　I have heard that guilty creatures sitting at a play
　　　　Have by the very cunning of the scene
　　　　Been struck so to the soul that presently
　　　　They have proclaimed their malefactions.
　　　　For murder,
DMITRY. *(Waving looking around) No!* Murder, *no!!*
GABE.   Though it have no tongue, will speak
　　　　With most miraculous organ. I'll have these players
　　　　Play something like the murder of my father
　　　　Before mine uncle. I'll observe his looks.
　　　　I'll tent him to the quick. If a' do blench,
　　　　I know my course. I'll have grounds
　　　　More relative than this. The play's the thing
　　　　Wherein I'll catch the conscience of the king.
(Gabe has backed Dmitry up against his car, his foil against Dmitry's neck. Dmitry, clutching his cap, terrified, shaking, suddenly recognizes the words; smiles in recognition. Takes a beat.)
DMITRY. *(Pointing at Gabe.)* Hamlet. *(Gabe smiles.)* S'good. Is good, very good. Hamlet. *(Gabe whips back the sword, bows with a flourish.)*
GABE.   I humbly thank you, well, well.
(Dmitry is beaming, as if caught in a movie.)
DMITRY. *(Pleased, self-conscious.)* Well. Yes.
GABE. Give me your pardon, sir. I have done you wrong.
DMITRY. *(Smiling.)* Yes.
GABE.   But pardon't, as you are a gentleman.

> This presence knows, and you must needs have heard,
> How I am punished with a sore distraction.
> What I have done
> That might your nature, honor, and exception
> Roughly awake, I here proclaim was madness.

DMITRY. *(Nodding.)* Yes. Yes.

GABE. Go to, I'll no more on't. Aye, so, good-bye to you.

(Dmitry watches him walk around to the driver's seat.)

DMITRY. Good-bye to you. Hamlet. *(Gabe gets in his car as Dmitry turns and looks back at his crashed cab. Sadly.)* Shitfuck. Shitfuck my taxicab. *(Dmitry shuffles off. Gabe starts up the car. Reaches in for his piece of pizza, highly pleased with himself, pumped up and confident for his performance.)*

GABE. Now I am alone.

(He stuffs the pizza into his mouth and keeps talking.)

> O, what a rogue and peasant slave am I.

(Lights start to fade.)

> Is it not monstrous that this player here …

Scene 5

A man and a woman, laughing offstage, enter. Caitlin is a librarian, an intellectual, her clothes a little disheveled, artsy, wears glasses; not at all fashion conscious. Zack is younger, a plumber, good looking, a local small town guy's guy; solid; wears jeans, work boots, Carhart jacket. They have gotten into a silly state, Caitlin particularly. She is charming in an offhanded Annie Hall kind of way. He finds her intriguing, if odd. Each feels flattered by the other's attention.

CAITLIN. Ahh, that's funny. *(She wipes tears of laughter from her eyes. Puts a hand on her stomach.)* My stomach hurts. My pizza hurts.

ZACK. We should do this again.

CAITLIN. Oh wait till it's over till you say that. *(He gets up his nerve and gives her a quick kiss, testing the waters. Adjusting her glasses.)* Gee. God. Wow. *(Seeing her response, he kisses her again, more passionately. Recovering.)* Zack. Well! What a surprise.

ZACK. So. Let's get to it.

CAITLIN. To what? Oop, you caught me off guard there. One little glass of wine, and I'm ... I never drink, you see. I don't drink. One glass ... *(She makes a hand gesture to indicate she's over the edge.)*

ZACK. You sure you can drive?

CAITLIN. Oh yeah. I mean I *can't* drive but I can't drive now as well as I never can. Can't. Ha! *(Laughs.)*

ZACK. *(Amused.)* You're ready.

CAITLIN. Ready, Freddy. *(As she goes to open the door he reaches over her shoulder and opens the door for her.)*

ZACK. You're loose, you're relaxed, you're adorable.

CAITLIN. *(Giggling.)* Really? *(She gets in as he goes around to the passenger side. She rolls her eyes to herself, in delight, anticipation.)* Hokay. I'm loose, I'm relaxed, I'm adorable. *(She flexes her fingers in preparation as he gets into the passenger seat.)* This is really very nice of you, Zack.

ZACK. It's nothing.

CAITLIN. It's not nothing, nothing it's not. It's something, I appreciate. Not many people would do this. Not many people would *brave* this. Okay. *(She takes a breath, turns the key, starts the car.)* You realize, don't you, that you're taking your life in your hands. I mean, you're putting your life in my hands.

ZACK. I trust you.

CAITLIN. It's not a question of trust. Trust has nothing to do with it. Here we go.

ZACK. You're doing great.

CAITLIN. Oh I'm fine on these little back roads.

ZACK. You have a very sexy mouth.

CAITLIN. *(Thrilled.)* Really? Thanks. You know, Zack, I've always thought of you as ... well ...

ZACK. What?

CAITLIN. I don't know. I certainly never thought I was your type. At all. I've always liked you. I've always thought you were good with your hands *(Embarrassing herself.)* I mean, when you fixed my sink, my plumbing. You seemed very … skilled, and … well, cool. Cool is the best word. And I am not. Basically, I'm pretty boring. I'm very smart but I'm boring. And for one thing, I'm considerably older than you.

ZACK. I've always liked older women.

CAITLIN. How many? How many older women have you always liked?

ZACK. I've always had my eye on you.

CAITLIN. Really?

ZACK. Yup. I'd see you jogging past my house. In your little outfits.

CAITLIN. Oh I don't have outfits. I just have … *clothes. (She looks over at him. He is smiling at her. She smiles, blushing.)* Mmm. Hokay, here we are. The Mass. Turnpike. I can't believe I asked you to do this. I can't believe you said yes, even for free beer and pizza.

ZACK. I'm relaxed. *(She looks at him.)*

CAITLIN. See? That's why I was trying to say. Cool. You're cool. *(She looks the other way and mimes taking a toll booth ticket. Smiling.)* Thank you. His smile was a little obsequious, don't you think, so it's about five minutes from here. *(She resumes driving.)* See, the problem is when there's no lane to pull over to, no breakdown lane? That's when it happens. When I'm stuck on the road, like a pinball in a groove, a guardrail hugging me from the right and I can't pull over. You're ready to take the wheel, right?

ZACK. You're gonna do just fine.

CAITLIN. *(Chattily, merrily, thoroughly enjoying herself.)* I'm not going to do just fine, I tell you that right now. I'm going to freak out. I haven't been back here in two years. Not since it happened. Now it takes me six hours to drive to Boston on back roads instead of two and a half. Did you know that one out of eight women have panic attacks? One out of eight. That's a lot of panic. I know it's psychological at this point. I know it's all in my head but I can't control it, ooo could you take your hand off my thigh please? I like your hand, it's just a little distracting. It's like the road freezes in a freeze frame, things stop moving as a video, and my mind jams into this … ozone … *warp* and it's *exhausting* like I'm towing the car with my brain and I can't breathe and I get disconnected from my body and I think I'll pass out. I never *have* passed out but I think

I will. If there's a breakdown lane, it doesn't happen; if there isn't one, it's … God, it's indescribably awful. Zack could you please stop chewing on my ear; it's kind of noisy. Maybe you'd like to come by later. *(She can't believe her audacity.)* The weird thing, I'm more afraid of the fear than I am of actually getting into a car crash.

ZACK. *(Pulling back from her.)* It's not going to happen again. You're over it.

CAITLIN. *(Still chatty, still buoyantly happy.)* I'm not over it. You're going to have to take the wheel at some point. You know it's recently occurred to me, maybe it's not so strange, to have a panic attack in this situation. Maybe something in my brain knows something I don't know; maybe it's protecting me and being very sensible, very rational. I mean, up until this century human beings didn't go faster than, what, five miles an hour, unless they were flung up on an ox or a horse or something, pitched out a castle window. For centuries, for millennia, humans have traveled very, very slowly. When you think about it, going sixty miles an hour, going *forty* miles an hour is a profoundly *unnatural* thing to do. *Insanely* dangerous. Maybe some part of my brain realizes this and says what the fuck are you doing out in this little tinny shitty metal box that can crumple like gum foil in an instant, flying, hurtling through space alongside of hundreds of other people in little tinny metal boxes many of whom are complete idiots, people who willingly kept Reagan in office for eight years, *morons* entrusted with these death machines simply by virtue of having passed a multiple choice test they can take over and over and over until they pass? It's insane. Really, people have panic attacks in very logical places — elevators, airplanes, cars — dangerous places. Maybe it's not panic, maybe it's preservation of the species, common sense, it's "Get your body out of here. This is a very, very *stupid* place for you to be."

ZACK. *(Nervous now.)* Hm.

CAITLIN. You know it's curious, they say money and sex are the key issues in a relationship. I think driving is more important; a couple's dynamic in a car. A car is more of a hotbed for emotions than a bed. I could never go out with a bad driver. I have broken up with guys because they're horrible drivers. If I'm going to be happy with a man I have to feel like I can lie down and put my head on his lap while he's at the wheel and not worry; not worry that he's not watching the road closely, not concentrating. I have to feel secure that he's driving competently, *defensively*. Give me safety points on a guy's driving record over Kurt Russell's thighs any day. Okay, we're getting close. There's a stretch up here very soon; no breakdown lane, a long monotonous guardrail, pressing in from the side. Oppressive, looming, encroaching, dominating, paralyzing, you ready? *(No response.)* Zack, are you ready?

ZACK. Uh ...

CAITLIN. You okay?

ZACK. Well ...

CAITLIN. *(Still in high spirits, totally relaxed.)* It's about to happen, I can feel it. You can't imagine all the things I've tried to combat it. Counting backwards, deep yoga breathing, bringing a stuffed animal with me and having him talk to me in an Indian dialect, telling me the life stories of all his fellow villagers ... *oh no ... (Caitlin freezes up, looks sick, as if she has vertigo, as if she's racing at an ungodly speed)* It's happening ... it's happening ... Zack ...? *(No response. Not able to move.)* Zack...?

ZACK. I don't think ...

CAITLIN. *(Quickly.)* You don't think what?

ZACK. I don't think ...

CAITLIN. Take the wheel.

ZACK. I can't.

CAITLIN. Take the wheel!

ZACK. I can't!

CAITLIN. Take the goddamned wheel!!! *(She takes her hands off the wheel and Zack reaches over and grabs it. She looks like she has stopped breathing. He looks terrified; grips the wheel, staring out at the road.)* Hold on! Hold on!

ZACK. *(Looks like he's in pain.)* I'm ... Caitlin, I'm losing it ...

CAITLIN. Well find it! *Find* it!!

ZACK. I'm ... I've never ... FUUUUUUCK!!

CAITLIN. We can pull over soon, oh, God, I hate this, I hate this, we can pull over soon.

ZACK. *(Quietly.)* Shit ...!

CAITLIN. Don't let go, Zack, don't let go, there's a rest area up ahead, pretty soon ... pretty soon ... pretty soon ... *(She sudden-*

ly grabs the wheel, turns it to the right and they pull over. She stops the car. Zack collapses back into his seat. They are now both breathing hard, in a sweat, exhausted.) Oh my *God.* What happened?

ZACK. I ...

CAITLIN. What happened to you, Zack?

ZACK. I don't know, I don't know.

CAITLIN. What?

ZACK. All those things you were saying ... The guardrail ... looming, oppressive ... Caitlin, I've never ... hurtling through space, I ... that was horrible.

CAITLIN. Yeah.

ZACK. *Horrible.* I'm sorry.

CAITLIN. I'm sorry. I didn't mean to talk you into ... my anxieties.

ZACK. My body is shaking.

CAITLIN. *(Knowingly.)* Yeah.

ZACK. Jesus. *(Pause.)*

CAITLIN. *(Disappointed.)* You know what this means.

ZACK. What?

CAITLIN. We can never go out. You and I. We can never date.

ZACK. How are we gonna get out of here?

CAITLIN. How disappointing.

ZACK. I can't go back on that highway.

CAITLIN. *(No problem.)* We'll hitch.

ZACK. Hitch?

CAITLIN. Hitch. It's nothing. I do it all the time.

ZACK. Man ...

CAITLIN. Do you think if you were in the driver's seat, you could drive?

ZACK. No. Maybe. How close is the next exit?

CAITLIN. Seven miles. Exactly. There's a Burger King there. A phone. An Asian guy named Mike whose mother lives in LA and can't make left turns.

ZACK. No. No. I can't. We'll never make it.

CAITLIN. No. We'll never make it. *(She sighs.)* What a shame. *(They look away in opposite directions as lights fade.)*

28

Scene 6

A young father is driving his son, dressed in a Halloween costume, from house to house for trick or treat. He speaks to his wife on a car phone each time the boy gets out. The boy is dressed as a ghost, covered with a sheet with eye holes cut out. It's important that the boy be very quiet, self-contained, calm. At the top of the scene the father is alone in the car, waiting for his son, watching him intently with binoculars.

RICK. He's knocking again. There's three other kids with him. Uh ... let's see, the Ninja Turtle I've seen before, the Spiderman, they're a team, and that's ... I don't know ... he's covered with number 10 tin cans, might be the Tin Man from *The Wizard of Oz*, might be a recycling center, *(Scanning the area with his binoculars.)* no witches, no witches ... huh? Not yet. Not yet. *Now.* Yeah. Bowls of looks like candy corn and ... miniature candy bars, Mounds bars I think, way to score, Marcus. He's okay, he's okay. He's waiting, he's waiting ... he's standing there with his bag, God he looks cute. Now it's his turn. He's taking a handful of candy corn. He's taking another handful. Oh Christ, he's going for another handful. She's putting two Mounds bars in his bag ... oh, no, I don't believe it ... he's going for more corn, Irene, he's going for more candy corn. This is unbelievable. Unbelievable. No, I won't, I won't ... I won't say anything. Irene, relax, relax. I'm not going to get on his case, I can't believe that woman is being so nice, he made a major dent in her supply, Jesus. I know he likes candy corn, that doesn't ... yes, he's six years old. Yup, *his* night. He's having a positive experience, Irene, he's having a purely positive experience. She's smiling. She is waving and closing the door. Okay, they're scattering. Here he comes. *(He hangs up and his son appears. Gets into the back seat of the car and intently studies the contents in his bag. Rick starts up the car.)* Okay? *(No response. Enthusiastically.)* Okay. So what'd you get? Marcus? *(Marcus is tak-*

ing out a fistful of candy corn.)
MARCUS. Candy.
RICK. Candy! Yes! All right. *(They drive in silence as Marcus brings his hand around under the sheet to get the candy corn to his mouth.)* You couldn't spare a Mounds bar, could you, pal? *(Marcus digs in his bag and hands his father a Mounds bar.)* Thanks. *(He unwraps and eats it.)* You know, my father used to love Mounds bars. They were his favorite candy. *(Marcus keeps eating candy corn, under the sheet.)* You okay, Marcus? Marcus, you okay?
MARCUS. Yup.
RICK. Having a good time? Not too hot in there? *(They both eat candy. Marcus takes a piece of candy corn and sticks it through one of his eyeholes to eat it.)* Okay. Next stop. Have fun. *(Rick stops the car and Marcus gets out and exits. Rick is immediately on the phone again while looking through binoculars.)* Hi. The corner of Shaler Lane and Mount Auburn. Yeah. The big green house. No, the green one. It's fine. Irene, it's fine. There's a big pumpkin in the window, all lit up. Why would they have a pumpkin all lit up if they weren't nice people? Huh? What? You're kidding, just now? Wait a minute, wait a minute, you opened the door, you gave them candy and he squirted you in the face with a lemon? How could he squirt you with a lemon? Oh yeah, one of those plastic things. What's he dressed as? He *is* a lemon? Hold on. Yeah, it's an older man, he looks very nice, he's wearing a cardigan sweater, he's fine. Uh … peanuts. Yup. In the shell. Too late. They're in the bag with the candy, we'll sort them later. He squirted you in the eyes, sweetheart, are you okay? Jesus. What a little asshole. What a little prick. You didn't take it away from him? Hold on, hold on, he's coming. Bye. *(Marcus gets in the back seat. Rick starts up the car.)* Hey, Marcus. How'd it go? What'd you get this time? Marcus, what'd you get? *(Marcus nibbles at one candy corn after another through an eyehole, his mouth up to it.)*
MARCUS. Peanuts.
RICK. Peanuts. Mmm. You know we can separate the peanuts from the candy when we get home, sometimes they get kind of messy all together.
MARCUS. *(Unintelligibly.)* Un ooth.
RICK. What? What'd you say?

MARCUS. Un oooth.

RICK. Uncouth?

MARCUS. *(Pulling an eyehole down to his mouth and speaking through it.)* That man only had one tooth.

RICK. One tooth! Ah. Well. You know why that could be. That could be because he ate too much candy. And, he didn't take care of his teeth. He didn't brush them twice a day and floss, and he ate too much candy corn so the sugar finally ate up all of his teeth except the one tooth which survived because he ate his vegetables but not enough vegetables. What do you think of that theory, Marcus? *(Silence as Marcus keeps chewing, nibbling, sucking on candy corn.)* Marcus, do you have any more Mounds bars back there in that great big bag of yours? You could lend me? I'll pay you back. *(Marcus hands him another candy bar.)* Thanks. *(Sees a witch on the sidewalk.)* Oops, Marcus, why don't you look that way, that way over there. That's very interesting, don't you think, over there? *(Marcus looks over, thereby not seeing the witch.)*

MARCUS. What?

RICK. That ... bush. In the dark. Interesting. *(The witch has passed. Rick stops the car.)* Hokay. Here we go! Go get 'em! *(Marcus gets out. Exits. Rick is on the phone, while watching Marcus.)* Hi. We just passed a witch but he didn't see her. I think she's headed toward you. How're your eyes? Have you rinsed them out? What the fuck did that little twerp put in that lemon, some chemical cleaning fluid. He's knocking on the door, Jesus, he's gonna pound the door down. What a fist. The doorbell? Okay. *(While she answers her doorbell, he stares forward through the windshield, lost in thought; perhaps pondering his childhood Halloweens, his father. He unwraps the candy bar Marcus gave him and starts to eat it. Marcus opens the back door for the lemon who gets in, and then Marcus gets in.)* So. How'd it go? *(Rick starts the car. Looks in the rear mirror. Sees the lemon, is completely startled.)* Jesus Christ! What's going on?

MARCUS. He wants to ride.

RICK. He wants to ride? Where? Why? Where are his parents? Marcus? *(Marcus is looking in the lemon's bag, checking out his candy. Rick picks up the phone, presses redial. In low hushed tones.)* He's in the car! He's in the car! The lemon. The *lemon*, he's in the back seat. Yes, with Marcus. I don't know, I don't know, he got in

31

with him, whatshouldIdo? WhatshouldIdo? Yeah. "Sunkissed;" on his face, on his head, it says "Sunkissed." What a nightmare. I'm being hijacked by a lemon. *(The lemon is now making weird noises, making Marcus giggle.)* He's making weird noises. Not lemon noises, what noises do lemons make? Shit, what if he squirts Marcus? Marcus is laughing. Laughing. I don't know, he thinks he's funny. He thinks fruit is funny, hysterical. I can't act upset, it'll freak Marcus out. What if he squirts me while I'm driving, I'll be blinded. No, if I stop they're gonna get out together, should I go with them, whatshouldIdo? *(Addressing the kids.)* So. How's it going back there? Good crop, in Florida? Was it a good crop in Florida this year, Mr. Lemon, good lemon crop, not too much frost, too many pesticides? *(The lemon's weird noises get a little louder.)* Uh-huh. Just make sure no juice drips out of you, you understand? No juice because this car is allergic to juice … it rusts … very quickly … so if you do, drip any juice, *anywhere,* I'll have to make lemonade out of you, understand?

MARCUS. Dad, stop.

RICK. I'm being friendly. I'm giving him a ride.

MARCUS. Stop the car!

RICK. Oh. The car. *(Rick stops the car. Marcus and the lemon get out.)* Okay. I'll watch from here. I'll watch you both from here, so if anything happens, if anybody does anything, pulls anything, I'll see it. From here. Okay. *(They exit, holding hands. Rick is on the phone in an instant.)* They're holding hands. They're walking up the front porch together holding hands. Jesus Christ, Marcus and the lemon, what a nightmare. No, he's not holding a lemon, I don't see any weapon, I don't know where he keeps it. He's holding a bag and he's holding Marcus. Oh my God. Oh my God. There's a witch. There's a witch … she's … shit! She's turning up … she's going … he doesn't see her … Irene … *(Rick leaps out of the car, runs offstage. After ten seconds the lemon enters and goes and sits in the car, followed by the witch who carries a broomstick, followed by Marcus. All three kids sit very quietly in the back seat eating candy. Marcus holds up a Tootsie Roll pop and unwraps it as Rick enters carrying a beer. He stands on the sidewalk, looks at the kids, expressionless; emotionally spent, takes a couple of swigs of beer. Gets in the car, moving the broomstick, which is in his*

32

way. Starts up the car. Drives. There is total silence except for suck-ing and chewing sounds. The stick of Marcus' Tootsie Roll pop sticks out of his eyehole. After a while, Rick stops, gets out, and opens the door to the back seat. Marcus gets out first and walks past him off-stage as the witch gets out, reaches into her bag, gives Rick a candy bar and hops away. He stares down at it. Looks up to see the lemon with his hand way down in his bag. Rick steps back, prepared to deal with being squirted, prepared to wrestle. The lemon pulls out a candy bar, gives it to Rick and follows the other kids offstage. Rick, stunned, walks around back to his seat, holding the candy. He gets on the phone. In a daze.) It's me. Everything's fine. I'm sorry. I'm sorry. I'm sorry. Everything's okay. He's fine. Yuh. *(As if in a dream.)* They tipped me. The lemon. The witch. They tipped me. *(Pause.)* Irene ... Next year ... next year, Marcus is walking. *(Lights fade as he takes a bite of candy.)*

ACT TWO

Scene 1

It's late — late night. Two street guys from Philly are in the car. Marty, a big baby, wired and anxious (has taken speed), is driving. He is terrified, singing to himself, drumming his fingers manically on the steering wheel. Dean, extremely cool, tough, potentially dangerous, is asleep, arms folded across his chest. When he speaks, Dean takes his time, often pausing first.

MARTY. You awake? Dean. *(Pause.)* Dean. *(Pause.)* Dean.
DEAN. *(Stirring.)* Huh?
MARTY. You're awake! Man, it's dark out here. It is *really* dark. *(Pause.)* Scared? Hey. Dean.
DEAN. Huh?
MARTY. You scared? *(No response.)* I was just thinking. *(Pause)*
DEAN. Where are we?
MARTY. Don't ask me, man. We are somewhere *dark.* We are somewhere intensely dark. What do you think, couple hours till daylight? 'nother couple hours?
DEAN. I don't know.
MARTY. You don't know? You don't have a watch?
DEAN. Did I have a watch before?
MARTY. Before when? *(Dean looks at him.)* Oh. That's cool. *(Pause.)* Jesus Christ. We are the only ones on the road. We are the only ones out on the road in all of Nevada. *(Pause.)* You're not scared.
DEAN. Turn on the radio.
MARTY. Radio? Radio, out here? You kidding? You turn on the radio all you're gonna hear is dark. We're not driving through

space. We're driving through dark. Through dark to light.

DEAN. *(Grimacing.)* My mouth.

MARTY. *(Drumming his fingers.)* Destination light.

DEAN. 'T's rotten.

MARTY. Your mouth is rotten? You're not gonna freak out on me again. Are you? Gonna freak out on me?

DEAN. *(Moving his tongue around.)* My whole mouth.

MARTY. I hope not. I hope you don't freak out on me again. That was weird. That was so weird, man. I couldn't take that again.

DEAN. There any water?

MARTY. Water? No. Nope.

DEAN. Soda?

MARTY. We're outa soda. Outa soda, outa beer. Nada. Nada nada.

DEAN. Shit. *(Pause.)* Got any gum?

MARTY. Gum? No. No gum.

DEAN. Life saver?

MARTY. No. *(Pause. Tension. Brightly.)* I got some toothpaste.

DEAN. Toothpaste?

MARTY. Under your seat.

DEAN. What's it doing there?

MARTY. Lives there.

DEAN. You don't care it'll melt?

MARTY. Dean. Toothpaste comes melted. *(Dean reaches down and takes it out. Takes off the cap.)*

DEAN. You got a toothbrush?

MARTY. No.

DEAN. You got toothpaste, no toothbrush?

MARTY. I don't have a toothbrush right now. *(Dean studies him.)* Sometimes I have one. I've had toothbrushes, I don't have one now. *(Dean squeezes a little out; carefully puts a dab in his mouth.)* Yeah. That was weird when you freaked out. Sudden like that. I thought you were gonna tear the car apart. I thought you were going to rip the roof off. Geez Louise. *(Dean sucks on the toothpaste.)*

DEAN. How old is this toothpaste?

MARTY. Huh?

DEAN. How old is this toothpaste?

MARTY. It's not old. Young. Toothpaste doesn't get old. I was thinking. You know how when you run fast, really fast, so fast you hear your heart pounding in your ears? Pounding. That's what it's like. Driving out here. Out in the middle of fucking nowhere. In the dark. All you hear are your thoughts. Pounding, in your ears. Dean. Do you believe in God?

DEAN. *(Verging on getting upset.)* There's no fucking water?

MARTY. To rinse?

DEAN. Yeah.

MARTY. No.

DEAN. Nothing to drink?

MARTY. No. There was, but ... it got drunk. *(Pause.) You* drank some of it. A lot of it. You did. Drink. Three cans at least. Three bottles. Minimum. I packed. Paid for. That's cool.

DEAN. We got a problem.

MARTY. Just swallow.

DEAN. Swallow.

MARTY. Swallow.

DEAN. I can't swallow.

MARTY. Spit it out then.

DEAN. *(Shaking his head.)* Marty ...

MARTY. Roll down your window and spit it out.

DEAN. You don't understand. I have no saliva. *(Pause.)*

MARTY. *(Cheerfully promoting it.)* It's spearmint. That's refreshing. It's natural. Please don't freak out on me again. Not now. Not here.

DEAN. What's natural?

MARTY. That toothpaste. It's organic.

DEAN. Organic. You can't believe organic.

MARTY. It's from Maine.

DEAN. Organic is a giant lie. What, they harvest it? Like a crop? Harvest toothpaste out of the ground? Off a tree? It's just another of their big fucking lies.

MARTY. *(Acquiescing, scared.)* You're right.

DEAN. Something doesn't age, it's not organic. It's immortal.

MARTY. I'm sorry. You're right. *(Pause.)* I'm sorry. *(Pause.)*

DEAN. We have a serious problem. We gotta stop.

MARTY. Dean, we can't stop.

DEAN. We gotta find some liquid.

MARTY. We're in the desert. There is no liquid. The desert is the opposite of liquid. There's snakes out there. I'm not stopping.

DEAN. *(About to explode.)* Marty …

MARTY. Just relax.

DEAN. There's gotta be liquid out there.

MARTY. Think pleasant thoughts.

DEAN. Something wet. Anything wet. *(Dean leans forward.)*

MARTY. Look out the window.

DEAN. I'm looking out the window.

MARTY. You're looking at the floor.

DEAN. I'm looking at my *MOUTH!!*

MARTY. You're free, Dean.

DEAN. Aarhn …

MARTY. *(Desperately trying to calm him down.)* You're free. *Free.*
Out on the open road. You made it. We've been talking about this
for years. Coming out here. We did it. Finally. We left. You're not
back there any more. Philly is 2,000 miles away. No probation
officer. No Darlene. You're here. Free. *(Reaches for a word he has
never said in his life.)* Rejoice. *(Pause.)*

DEAN. *(Testing the word.)* Rejoice.

MARTY. On the road! *(Pause.)* Destination light. *(Pause.)*

DEAN. *(Settling back.)* Destination light.

MARTY. *(Hitting the steering wheel.)* Fuckin' A! *(Dean, temporar-
ily calmed, stares out his window. Marty holds the steering wheel
tightly, leans forward a tad, glancing nervously over at Dean.)*

Scene 2

*A dance. Again, the actress need not necessarily be a dancer.
She just needs to move freely and with uninhibited enthu-
siasm for her upcoming weekend escape. In the dark, we
hear a self-help relaxation tape. Lights come up to reveal a
woman in a suit and high heels driving home from work,
listening to the tape. She is horribly stressed, trying to follow the instructions on the tape but just getting more and
more stressed in traffic. She pulls into her driveway and
mimes ejecting the tape. Turns on the radio and zooms*

through static and stations until she finds the right song, which she turns up. ("Send Me On My Way"* by Rusted Root works well.) The dance begins — a combination of taking off her constraining work clothes and putting on athletic gear to go rock climbing for the weekend. She goes in and out of her house, dancing to the music in and around the car, bringing gear — a backpack, climbing rope, boots, etc. Has spandex tights on under the skirt; puts on sweatshirt, bandanna, sunglasses, cap. As she throws things into the back seat she dances humorously with broad silly movements, letting down her hair, loosening up. The freer and more exaggerated the movements the better. She should be gleeful and silly, dying to get out of town, out of her work mode. By the end, she is in the driver's seat, tossing an apple in the air and taking a bite, or drinking a swig of water from her water bottle. On the road.

Scene 3

The car appears to be empty, but Queenie, a homeless woman dressed in large overcoat, scarves and hat pulled down over much of her face, is sleeping in the back seat. A loudspeaker from a public utility truck blares.

LOUDSPEAKER. Street cleaning! Street cleaning! Move all cars from the odd-numbered side of the road!
QUEENIE. *(Lying down.)* Oh my God. Not again.
LOUDSPEAKER. All cars from the odd numbered side of the road will be tagged and towed!
QUEENIE. EXCUSE ME!!
LOUDSPEAKER. Street cleaning!
QUEENIE. Hel-LOOOO! People are SLEEPING!
LOUDSPEAKER. Street cleaning!

* See Special Note on Songs and Recordings on copyright page.

QUEENIE. This is inexcusable.

LOUDSPEAKER. Move all cars from the odd-numbered side of the road! All cars from the odd-numbered side of the road will be tagged and towed!

QUEENIE. I'll tag and tow you, buddy! SHUT UP!

LOUDSPEAKER. Street cleaning! Street cleaning! *(Queenie sits up abruptly, wrapped in an old blanket, looks out the window at someone walking past on the sidewalk.)*

QUEENIE. *(Angrily.)* What are you looking at? What are you looking at? Don't you dare screw your face at this car Mister "Oh I'm so innocent!" Mister "I just got out of bed put on these plaid pants and my wife made me breakfast!" Wipe it off, meatbrain-head, wipe it off! *(After glowering at him as he passes, she wraps the blanket more tightly around her. It's freezing cold. She studies the windowpane. Wipes a circle in the steamed window. Leans back. Breathes again; makes another design. Sits back. Makes a discovery in her mouth we don't quite get. She makes a face.)* Holy Toledo. *(She puts her finger up in the roof of her mouth. Touches something.)* What in blazes …? *(As she focuses on the object in her mouth, Philip, a wealthy man in his forties, approaches. Dressed for work in a handsome overcoat, silk scarf, gloves and hat, he carries a briefcase in one hand and a coffee to go and a muffin in the bag in the other. He is wearing no shoes. He walks slowly over to the car. Emotionally devastated, with zero energy, he stands by the car, in a daze. He opens the door, tosses in the briefcase, and gets into the driver's seat. Sits still, saying nothing.)* You're late. *(He doesn't look back at her. Knows she's there.)* Where ya been, ya big lug? *(No response.)* All's I can say is you're lucky you got security, you are one lucky hamburger. No charge, but … I gotta say, I got a few complaints. *(No response. Yelling at him.)* A few complaints!

PHILIP. *(Docilely.)* Yeah.

QUEENIE. Yeah. *(Pause.)* No charge. *(Pause.)* You look trashed, Ph'lip. You look like the film caught on fire. AND you left your keys in the ginition. Again. You must have wondered where they were. Like, gone into your brain and said, "ExCUSE me, there's some inforMATION in here." Duh. *(Pause.)* I gotta go.

PHILIP. *(Still staring forward.)* Don't go.

QUEENIE. I gotta.

PHILIP. Where?

QUEENIE. Same place always. Work, jerk.

PHILIP. Work?

QUEENIE. You're not gonna believe ... this fisherman's lozenger, in my mouth when I went to sleep? It was there this morning, all the way later, lying on the roof of my mouth. Like a little child, curled up. Safe. *(Pause.)* I went to sleep, it was there. Woke up; still there.

PHILIP. Huh.

QUEENIE. So what happened on Good Morning, America? She finally leave?

PHILIP. *(Slowly.)* Yes. She did. She left me.

QUEENIE. She leave a note?

PHILIP. Unfortunately.

QUEENIE. That was courteous. You know, my elbow. I think it got turned around in my sleep. I woke up, it was facing the other way.

PHILIP. She left a long note. They always do. I inspire length. In good-bye notes. *(He takes a sip of coffee.)*

QUEENIE. I'm outa here.

PHILIP. Stay. You want a muffin?

QUEENIE. What kinda muffin?

PHILIP. Morning glory.

QUEENIE. Morning glory. You shittin' me?

PHILIP. That's what the girl called it. *(He turns for the first time and hands her the bag with the muffin in it. She takes it out and studies it. He turns back and faces forward again.)*

QUEENIE. Morning glory. Somebody had a idea. *(She starts eating it. He takes another sip of coffee.)*

PHILIP. I can't sleep in that apartment. Tonight. Alone. I can't.

QUEENIE. Call me nuts, I think someone parked a carrot in here. *(He takes another sip.)*

PHILIP. Do you live alone, Queenie?

QUEENIE. Excuse me, I live with you.

PHILIP. Oh. That's nice. That's ... good.

QUEENIE. Flatter yourself

PHILIP. We go way back, don't we, Queenie? How long have you been sleeping in my car?

QUEENIE. Halloween. And don't you think your boss is just going to maybe wonder where you are? Don't you think Mr. Hewlitt Packard is going to say, "Where is that Ph'lipwit, now that I need him?"

PHILIP. I can't go to work.

QUEENIE. Why in blazes not?

PHILIP. I can't. I can't. *(Pause.)* I have to go ... somewhere. I don't know where.

QUEENIE. Mm. *(She starts to go.)* Bye.

PHILIP. Wait. I'll turn on the heat. *(He starts up the car; turns on the heat. She stays.)* Do you have any family? Queen?

QUEENIE. I saw my grandmother cut up my grandfather. When I was a little girl. He came home, late, she knew where he'd been, she cut him up everywhere. I was screaming. *(She suddenly screams a blood-curdling scream, back in the memory.)* "Mama, *don't!* Don't do it! *Please don't!*" *(Philip is startled, spills his coffee.)* She took all his things, all his belongings, took them out back and made a big bonfire. Her friend, Gloria, tried to tell her how to do it, she said, "This is MY fire! *No one* is gonna tell me how to do *MY* fire!" She took two pairs of shoes, a pair of his shoes, put them on top, pointing in different directions.

PHILIP. Huh ...

QUEENIE. The firemen came. But it was too late. The shoes were gone. One one way; the other the other. *(Pause.)* I have a sister. *(Proudly.)* Beautiful Betty Moran.

PHILIP. Where does she live?

QUEENIE. Baltimore.

PHILIP. When was the last time you saw her?

QUEENIE. I don't know. *(She tries to remember. Sadly)* I don't know I ever did.

PHILIP. *(Starting to pick up.)* Let's go visit her.

QUEENIE. *Whoa.* I think this morning glory is going to my head.

PHILIP. She'll be glad to see you. *(He starts to pull out. She gets upset, looking out the window.)*

QUEENIE. Hold on, soldier! Not so fast!

PHILIP. South. We'll go south. To Baltimore.

QUEENIE. Hey, it's moving. *(Upset.)* Stop! Arrest that car! *(Queenie's head slowly goes back and forth as she watches things go by.)*

PHILIP. I'll buy you lunch.

QUEENIE. No!

PHILIP. I'll buy you dinner.

QUEENIE. No!

PHILIP. You can have my car.

QUEENIE. I don't like this!

PHILIP. You want to ride in front? You want to drive? *(He stops the car and looks back at her.)* Queenie, you want to drive?

QUEENIE. Are you crazy? *(Pause.)* We can't visit my sister.

PHILIP. Why not? Why can't we visit beautiful Betty Moran? Don't you think she'll be happy to see us? Don't you think she'll smile when she sees our faces? Don't you think that would be a nice unusual experience, to have someone smile when she sees you?

QUEENIE. What if we get there and she's just a pile of bad news?

PHILIP. She won't be.

QUEENIE. *(Frightened.)* She might be. There's ugly Eddie. I might get carsick. I might get homesick.

PHILIP. This is your home.

QUEENIE. *(Grabbing her stuff.)* I'm getting out.

PHILIP. Don't! *(Desperately grabbing her.)* Queenie, help! Help me. Where should we go? We could always make a suicide pact.

QUEENIE. *(Quickly.)* Hang a left.

PHILIP. Okay. *(He pulls out onto the road, makes a left.)* Now what?

QUEENIE. Hang a right.

PHILIP. There is no right.

QUEENIE. Sit tight. You're giving me a headache. *(Pause.)* I gotta idea.

PHILIP. What is it? *(She leans forward.)*

QUEENIE. We'll go till we run out of land.

PHILIP. Huh?

QUEENIE. We'll go till we run out of land.

PHILIP. Okay. That's a good idea. Okay. *(Calming down.)* Thanks, Queenie. Thanks. *(He takes a deep breath, a sigh.)*

QUEENIE. You forgot your shoes. *(He just keeps looking straight ahead.)* One good thing. It's warm. Least it's warm in here. *(Philip gazes forward as Queenie tilts her head and stares out the window. Lights fade.)*

Scene 4

In the dark, over music between scenes, there is sighing, moaning, lovemaking. Music fades out; moans fade out. Quiet.

HENRY. *(Exuberant.)* Wow! *(A dim blue light comes up, shows their silhouettes in the back seat of the car.)*
LISA. Could you ...?
HENRY. What?
LISA. Uh ... my shirt ... is twisted around your ...
HENRY. Oh. Okay. Sorry. Here.
LISA. Thanks.
HENRY. Better?
LISA. Yeah.
HENRY. *(Thrilled.)* God Lisa, that was wonderful, that was great.
LISA. *(Noncommittal.)* Mm.
HENRY. Wow. *(Pause.)*
LISA. *(Not pleased.)* I can't believe we did it in a car.
HENRY. *(Pleased.)* Yeah.
LISA. Our first time.
HENRY. Yeah.
LISA. We should have gone back to my apartment.
HENRY.. Why? This was ...
LISA. Could you move your foot?
HENRY. Sure. *(Pause.)* You okay?
LISA. *(Yes.)* Uh-huh.
HENRY. You don't sound okay.
LISA. I am. I just ... think we ... should have been in a bed.
HENRY. Well. Next time.
LISA. Mm.
HENRY. Was it ...?
LISA. Is my sock down there on the floor? My feet are kind of cold.
HENRY. Oh. *(Feeling in the dark.)* I think it's ... Is this it? No. Doesn't feel like a sock. Hm. *(Chuckling.)* I don't know what this

43

is. *(Lisa turns on the overhead lights.)*
LISA. I got it.
HENRY. Good. You're cold?
LISA. A little.
HENRY. Come here. *(He gently pulls her against him, holds her.)* You know, my parents tell me I was ... uh ... conceived in a car.
LISA. Your parents told you that?
HENRY. *(Chuckling.)* I don't know who else would tell me.
LISA. Really?
HENRY. Yup. Yes.
LISA. Oh.
HENRY. What do you think of that?
LISA. I think it's kind of ... cheap.
HENRY. Cheap?
LISA. Yeah.
HENRY. Cheap? It's not cheap. It's romantic.
LISA. I'm sorry but sex in a car is just not ... romantic.
HENRY. Yes it is. It's very romantic. *Very* romantic.
LISA. I can think of more romantic places.
HENRY. Like what? Where?
LISA. Like in a bed. A feather bed. A nice hotel. A little hideaway cabin with a fire going in the fireplace.
HENRY. *(Enthusiastically.)* Come on! A *car.* A car is ... how many people over the century have made out in cars. At scenic lookouts. At drive-ins.
LISA. Drive-ins are obsolete.
HENRY. Driving down a country road, pulling over, parking. Parking doesn't just mean, you know, parking your car. If you go parking with your girlfriend it's something else.
LISA. Yeah, when Eisenhower was president.
HENRY. Well. I don't know what to say. *(He starts putting on his shoes.)* I'm sorry. I'm sorry I subjected you to a horrible date.
LISA. It wasn't horrible.
HENRY. *(Simply.)* Lisa, I love you.
LISA. Henry ...
HENRY. I do.
LISA. You don't have to say that.
HENRY. But I do. Love you. For me not to say it, not to

acknowledge it, would be like not acknowledging a little rain cloud inside the car, pouring rain. There *isn't* one, but if there *were* one, it would be very odd not to comment on it. Actually, it feels kind of like a storm, in my system, these emotions, that I have for you. They're terribly distracting, I can't focus properly, can't do *anything* really without this constant disturbance, like a swarm of bees inside and outside me ... this tumultuous ... uh ... *obsession* with you. It's hard to describe. Sometimes, when I'm with you, Lisa, I feel like there are three people in the room: you, me and this ... tangle of emotions zooming around, wild patterns, protons, neutrons, racing, this sculpture that I happen to be carrying around inside me. You know I'm normally pretty witty, my friends think I'm *funny,* but when I'm with you my, I just, my tongue gets shipwrecked on my teeth. I have to say that it's not entirely *pleasant* being so completely uncontrollably smitten by you. There's actually quite a bit of pain involved that ... a *lot* of pain I can't do much about, but ... Lisa, you touch something so deep in me ... I felt it the instant I met you, I had to run out of the room. Your voice, your language, these phrases you come up with — "loaded for bear," "boarding-house reach" when you reached across me in the conference room for pizza, "boarding-house reach" I love that, I just ... how you talk, your eyes, your handwriting. Physically, I find you incredibly sexy but that's the least of it ... I love watching you watch things, I do, I could watch you watching things forever ... your sense of ... I'm babbling I know not very likely making much but ... if I can just at least try to express ... No one has ever made me feel the way that you do. I know, I realize it's *my* problem, I'm not dumping all this on you, I'm the one who has to deal with it, but I *am* in love with you. *(Pause.)* I guess we should go. *(He goes back to tying his shoes.)*

LISA. What kind of car?

HENRY. Huh?

LISA. What kind of car were you conceived in?

HENRY. '63 Ford Caravan.

LISA. Mm.

HENRY. I think I broke my glasses.

LISA. Oh no, the frames?

HENRY. *(Reaching down.)* A lens fell out. I got it. *(Pause.)*

LISA. I like your glasses.
HENRY. Mm. Well. *(He reaches for the door.)*
LISA. I'd like to spend the night with you here in the car.
HENRY. You would?
LISA. I would.
HENRY. I have a blanket in the back.
LISA. Mm. *(She snuggles up against him.)*

Scene 5

A family is taking a Sunday drive. Anne, the mother, relentlessly cheerful and upbeat, is driving. Gerald, the father, is in the passenger seat, head drooping as he stares at the road out of the tops of his eyes. Between them is Ruthie, thirteen, glasses, dressed in punk; woefully serious. In the back seat, Great Grannie is behind Anne; Jean-Luc, a French foreign exchange student, is behind Gerald; trapped between them is Terrence, a twelve-year-old boy, wearing a T-shirt and baseball cap. Everyone looks absolutely tortured except the mother.

ANNE. *Jean-Luc, ca va? Tu n'est pas trop chaud?*
JEAN-LUC. *Non, madame. Ca va tres bien, merci.*
ANNE. *Les arbres sont tres jolis, n'est-ce pas?*
JEAN-LUC. *Oui, madame.*
ANNE. *Tres jolis, mais pas assez rouge, je crois. On va trouver les feuilles vraiment rouges. Comme le feu. Tu va voir.*
JEAN-LUC. *Oui, madame.*
GERALD. *(Gently.)* Honey, I think you could pick it up.
ANNE. Pick what up?
GERALD. Your speed. You're going thirty in a fifty zone.
ANNE. Well. That leaves twenty for someone else.
GERALD. *(Smiling, diplomatically.)* I think that makes no sense.
ANNE. Gerald, you could make an effort to be pleasant. Great

Grannie? Great Grannie?

TERRENCE. She's asleep.

ANNE. What?

GERALD. She's asleep.

TERRENCE. She's the only person I know who can fart in her sleep.

ANNE. Terrence, you're mumbling again. Try to enunciate your words more carefully.

GERALD. *(Enunciating carefully.)* She's the only person he knows who can fart in her sleep.

ANNE. *(Sternly.)* Gerald …

GERALD. Just assisting communication. Is the parking brake on? *(Anne doesn't respond.)*

ANNE. There's a bag of apples in the back if anyone gets hungry. Nice crisp Macintosh apples from Taft Farm. And there's cider, too. Oh, what a beautiful day.

RUTHIE. Dad.

GERALD. What?

RUTHIE. Your elbow is practically inside me.

GERALD. Sorry. *(He adjusts his position. In spite of himself.)* This is torture.

ANNE. Gerald, this is not torture. Mankind suffers torture. Presently, daily. All over the planet, but never in the form of a Sunday country drive. *Jean-Luc, si tu veux ouvrir la fenetre tu peut.*

JEAN-LUC. *Merci, madame. (Grateful, Jean-Luc rolls down his window.)*

GERALD. Let's go home, sweetheart. I'm afraid this is a bad year for leaves.

ANNE. We just need to get a little farther north.

GERALD. Anne. You're driving more slowly than the leaves are turning. We'll never catch up to them.

ANNE. The farther north you go, the more colorful the leaves are.

GERALD. By the time we get north, it will be spring.

ANNE. Jean-Luc has never seen a New England fall, Gerald.

RUTHIE. *(Morosely.)* He's never seen a New England anything. He just got here yesterday.

GERALD. Look. There are some red leaves. That's a good tree, right there. Now we can go home.

ANNE. Where?

GERALD. Over there. It's red.

ANNE. It's not red. It's brown. Those are dried old oak leaves. Ruthie, how's your stomach?

RUTHIE. You don't want to know.

ANNE. So. *(Brightly.)* Right now, in Paris, Harriet is meeting her French family. She's on the *Rue St. Germaine,* wearing her new red beret, her new black shoes, meeting *Monsieur* and *Madame de Fleures* and their little dog, *Gaston.* Maybe they're out at a *patisserie,* having a *citronade,* a *gateaux des fraises.* While their son is here with us, his new American family, seeing the fall foliage.

TERRENCE. Smelling Great Grannie's killer farts.

GERALD. Terrence ...

TERRENCE. He can't understand what I'm saying.

ANNE. That's very rude. Very rude. You're being rude to Great Granni and you're being rude to Jean-Luc.

JEAN-LUC. *(Hearing his name.) Oui?*

ANNE. *Rien, Jean-Luc. C'est un tres joli jour, n'est-ce pas?*

JEAN-LUC. *Oui, madame.*

ANNE. *Un joli jour dans la campagne. (Anne whistles. No one moves as she reminisces.)* I remember when I was a little girl, fall was my favorite season. We'd go for long, wonderful country drives, sometimes up in Vermont, in New Hampshire, and we'd look at the trees, hillsides of gorgeous yellows and reds and oranges all ablaze. We'd buy maple syrup and pumpkins and bushels of apples. At home, we'd rake huge piles of leaves in the yard, huge mountains of leaves and jump in them and play for hours and hours. We didn't need malls or video games. I used to love to stand on the street and catch the falling leaves before they touched the ground. It wasn't easy because they'd flit back and forth on their way down. You'd hold your hands out and before you knew it, the leaf had flitted right through.

GERALD. *(Semi-comatose.)* Anne. We're slipping backwards. We're heading south.

ANNE. One day, when I was in high school, I had to catch twenty-five leaves, I told myself, twenty-five. It took me all afternoon. Finally, when I had twenty-five leaves I put them in a pot with some water and a little pinch of sugar and some herbs and some mustard and I put the pot on the stove at a low heat and stirred them with a long wooden spoon. And sang. Sang over the pot of leaves. And then I went out in the back yard and dug a hole in the ground and buried the leaves, way down deep, covering them with the moist black dirt, chanting some strange mythical syllables to make the boy I loved fall in love with me.

RUTHIE. Did it work?

ANNE. Yes, it did.

TERRENCE. Was it dad?

ANNE. Yes, it was. It was your father. He asked me out the next day. *(Gerald lifts his head slightly.)*

RUTHIE. I don't like the fall.

ANNE. No?

RUTHIE. I don't like fall leaves. I don't think leaves should be red and orange. It's unnatural. They should be green and healthy. A red leaf is a dying leaf. All those hillsides of leaves aflame yellow gold, red, it's all decay. A landscape of *decay. Death.* It's depressing. *(Silence.)*

ANNE. *(In a whole new tone; finally pissed off.)* I think they should have foreign exchange mothers. I think mothers should be allowed to go to other countries and have new families. New enthusiastic families. New husbands. New children. *(Silence.)*

RUTHIE. I'm sorry. I didn't ...

ANNE. *(Abruptly.)* It's all right.

GERALD. *(Touched.)* You never told me that story. About the leaves.

ANNE. No. *(Pause.)* I always thought if I told you that story the spell would be broken and you wouldn't love me any more. *(Silence. Ruthie looks over at her mother. Then speaks.)*

RUTHIE. *(Upset.)* Mom.

TERRENCE. *(Upset.)* Mom.

ANNE. What?

RUTHIE. You told him.

ANNE. So.

TERRENCE. You shouldn't have told him.

ANNE. Oh well.

RUTHIE. Now, the spell is broken.

ANNE. Maybe it is.

RUTHIE. You'll have to make a new spell. *Soon. Right away.*

ANNE. *(Still pissed off.)* I can't make a new spell. I don't know how. You can only make spells when you're young and innocent and full of hope and you act on instinct. And you're full of strange mythical syllables you don't understand. *(Ruthie starts sniffling.)* Ruthie. Are you crying? Sweetheart, you ate too many crepes. I told you you'd get a stomachache eating that many crepes. *(Ruthie keeps crying. Gets an idea.)*

RUTHIE. Stop the car.

ANNE. Are you going to be sick? *(Anne pulls over and stops the car, everyone swaying together to the car's movements.)* Gerald ... *(Gerald gets out so Ruthie can get out. He stretches as Ruthie goes around to the back to wake up Great Grannie.)*

GERALD. *(With relief.)* Ah. God.

ANNE. *(Looking under the seat.)* There's paper towel here somewhere.

RUTHIE. *(Loudly.)* Great Grannie.

ANNE. What are you doing, sweetheart?

RUTHIE. Great Grannie, wake up.

ANNE. Ruthie.

GREAT GRANNIE. *(Stirring.)* Are we here?

RUTHIE. We're here. I need your help.

GREAT GRANNIE. Oh. That's nice. *(Anne gets out of the car.)*

ANNE. *I'll* help you.

RUTHIE. No, thanks. Can you come with me? Please?

GREAT GRANNIE. Certainly. *(With great effort Great Grannie gets out of the car, stooped over. She holds her right arm up in front of her, her thumb has a nonstop tremor. Looking around.)* This isn't how I remember it.

ANNE. Are you warm enough? *(As Ruthie offers her support under her left arm, Jean-Luc jumps out of the car.)* Jean-Luc, qu'est-ce que tu fait?

JEAN-LUC. Je vais avec eux.

ANNE. Ruthie ... *(Jean-Luc comes around and assists Great Grannie on the other side. Great Grannie stares at him intently with curiosity as they start to exit.)*

RUTHIE. We'll just be in the woods. We won't be long.

ANNE. The woods? Gerald, go with them.

RUTHIE. No. Please. Let me follow *my* instincts.

GERALD. *(Gently, moved by Ruthie's intentions.)* They'll be fine.

ANNE. *Faite bien attention.*

JEAN-LUC. *Oui, madame.*

GREAT GRANNIE. *(Still staring at Jean-Luc.)* Are we related?

JEAN-LUC. *Je regrette, madame. Je ne parle pas anglais. (Great Grannie leans back, taken aback by his French; greatly surprised, fascinated. Ruthie, Great Grannie and Jean-Luc shuffle off. Anne stands outside the driver's seat; Gerald stands outside the passenger seat, and Terrence is silent in the back seat.)*

ANNE. Why do you always have to be in control? You're not happy unless you're in the driver's seat, behind the wheel.

GERALD. That's not true.

ANNE. Yes, it is.

GERALD. Maybe it is.

ANNE. The one time I drive, the one time I … set the pace, you're in a twisted state of torture.

GERALD. You're right.

ANNE. You've been acting like I've been feeding you slow burning asphalt for the last two hours.

GERALD. *(Sincerely.)* I'm sorry. *(Pause.)*

ANNE. I wonder what they're doing over there.

GERALD. I think they're chanting strange mythical syllables. With great facility. I can't imagine a more perfect threesome for the task.

TERRENCE. That's a nice tree over there.

ANNE. Where?

TERRENCE. Over there. The leaves are really yellow.

GERALD. Huh. That *is* a nice tree. *Very* pretty.

TERRENCE. That's the prettiest tree I've seen in a long time. *(Anne stares quietly at the tree. Gerald has come up behind her.)*

ANNE. Okay. We can go home. *(Lights fade.)*

PROPERTY LIST

Envelope with drawing on it (ELLEN)
Tweed jacket (MICHAEL)
Soup (ELLEN)
Bouquet of red roses (DANCER)
Four-subject notebook (SUZIE)
Study guide to *Moby Dick* (SUZIE)
Fat pink pen (SUZIE)
Dead chipmunk (JAY)
Jacket and backpack (HEIDIE)
Box with a slice of pizza (GABE)
Foil (GABE)
Car phone (RICK)
Binoculars (RICK)
Bag of candy (MARCUS) with:
        Mounds bars,
        candy corns
Tootsie Roll pop (MARCUS)
Beer (RICK)
Toothpaste (DEAN)
Climbing gear (DANCER) including:
        backpack
        climbing rope
        boots
        sweatshirt
        bandana
        sunglasses
        cap
        water bottle
Apple (DANCER)
Briefcase (PHILIP)
Coffee to go (PHILIP)
Muffin in a bag (PHILIP)
Glasses (HENRY)

SOUND EFFECTS

Car approaching
Car crash
Self-help relaxation tape
Zooming through radio stations
Loudspeaker

NEW PLAYS

★ **YELLOW FACE by David Henry Hwang.** Asian-American playwright DHH leads a protest against the casting of Jonathan Pryce as the Eurasian pimp in the original Broadway production of *Miss Saigon*, condemning the practice as "yellowface." The lines between truth and fiction blur with hilarious and moving results in this unreliable memoir. "A pungent play of ideas with a big heart." *—Variety.* "Fabulously inventive." *—The New Yorker.* [5M, 2W] ISBN: 978-0-8222-2301-6

★ **33 VARIATIONS by Moisés Kaufmann.** A mother coming to terms with her daughter. A composer coming to terms with his genius. And, even though they're separated by 200 years, these two people share an obsession that might, even just for a moment, make time stand still. "A compellingly original and thoroughly watchable play for today." *—Talkin' Broadway.* [4M, 4W] ISBN: 978-0-8222-2392-4

★ **BOOM by Peter Sinn Nachtrieb.** A grad student's online personal ad lures a mysterious journalism student to his subterranean research lab. But when a major catastrophic event strikes the planet, their date takes on evolutionary significance and the fate of humanity hangs in the balance. "Darkly funny dialogue." *—NY Times.* "Literate, coarse, thoughtful, sweet, scabrously inappropriate." *—Washington City Paper.* [1M, 2W] ISBN: 978-0-8222-2370-2

★ **LOVE, LOSS AND WHAT I WORE by Nora Ephron and Delia Ephron, based on the book by Ilene Beckerman.** A play of monologues and ensemble pieces about women, clothes and memory covering all the important subjects—mothers, prom dresses, mothers, buying bras, mothers, hating purses and why we only wear black. "Funny, compelling." *—NY Times.* "So funny and so powerful." *—WowOwow.com.* [5W] ISBN: 978-0-8222-2355-9

★ **CIRCLE MIRROR TRANSFORMATION by Annie Baker.** When four lost New Englanders enrolled in Marty's community center drama class experiment with harmless games, hearts are quietly torn apart, and tiny wars of epic proportions are waged and won. "Absorbing, unblinking and sharply funny." *—NY Times.* [2M, 3W] ISBN: 978-0-8222-2445-7

★ **BROKE-OLOGY by Nathan Louis Jackson.** The King family has weathered the hardships of life and survived with their love for each other intact. But when two brothers are called home to take care of their father, they find themselves strangely at odds. "Engaging dialogue." *—TheaterMania.com.* "Assured, bighearted." *—Time Out.* [3M, 1W] ISBN: 978-0-8222-2428-0

DRAMATISTS PLAY SERVICE, INC.
440 Park Avenue South, New York, NY 10016   212-683-8960   Fax 212-213-1539
postmaster@dramatists.com   www.dramatists.com

NEW PLAYS

★ **A CIVIL WAR CHRISTMAS: AN AMERICAN MUSICAL CELEBRA-TION by Paula Vogel, music by Daryl Waters.** It's 1864, and Washington, D.C. is settling down to the coldest Christmas Eve in years. Intertwining many lives, this musical shows us that the gladness of one's heart is the best gift of all. "Boldly inventive theater, warm and affecting." *–Talkin' Broadway.* "Crisp strokes of dialogue." *–NY Times.* [12M, 5W] ISBN: 978-0-8222-2361-0

★ **SPEECH & DEBATE by Stephen Karam.** Three teenage misfits in Salem, Oregon discover they are linked by a sex scandal that's rocked their town. "Savvy comedy." *–Variety.* "Hilarious, cliché-free, and immensely entertaining." *–NY Times.* "A strong, rangy play." *–NY Newsday.* [2M, 2W] ISBN: 978-0-8222-2286-6

★ **DIVIDING THE ESTATE by Horton Foote.** Matriarch Stella Gordon is determined not to divide her 100-year-old Texas estate, despite her family's declining wealth and the looming financial crisis. But her three children have another plan. "Goes for laughs and succeeds." *–NY Daily News.* "The theatrical equivalent of a page-turner." *–Bloomberg.com.* [4M, 9W] ISBN: 978-0-8222-2398-6

★ **WHY TORTURE IS WRONG, AND THE PEOPLE WHO LOVE THEM by Christopher Durang.** Christopher Durang turns political humor upside down with this raucous and provocative satire about America's growing homeland "insecurity." "A smashing new play." *–NY Observer.* "You may laugh yourself silly." *–Bloomberg News.* [4M, 3W] ISBN: 978-0-8222-2401-3

★ **FIFTY WORDS by Michael Weller.** While their nine-year-old son is away for the night on his first sleepover, Adam and Jan have an evening alone together, beginning a suspenseful nightlong roller-coaster ride of revelation, rancor, passion and humor. "Mr. Weller is a bold and productive dramatist." *–NY Times.* [1M, 1W] ISBN: 978-0-8222-2348-1

★ **BECKY'S NEW CAR by Steven Dietz.** Becky Foster is caught in middle age, middle management and in a middling marriage—with no prospects for change on the horizon. Then one night a socially inept and grief-struck millionaire stumbles into the car dealership where Becky works. "Gently and consistently funny." *–Variety.* "Perfect blend of hilarious comedy and substantial weight." *–Broadway Hour.* [4M, 3W] ISBN: 978-0-8222-2393-1

DRAMATISTS PLAY SERVICE, INC.
440 Park Avenue South, New York, NY 10016 212-683-8960 Fax 212-213-1539
postmaster@dramatists.com www.dramatists.com

NEW PLAYS

★ **AT HOME AT THE ZOO by Edward Albee.** Edward Albee delves deeper into his play THE ZOO STORY by adding a first act, HOMELIFE, which precedes Peter's fateful meeting with Jerry on a park bench in Central Park. "An essential and heartening experience." –*NY Times.* "Darkly comic and thrilling." –*Time Out.* "Genuinely fascinating." –*Journal News.* [2M, 1W] ISBN: 978-0-8222-2317-7

★ **PASSING STRANGE book and lyrics by Stew, music by Stew and Heidi Rodewald, created in collaboration with Annie Dorsen.** A daring musical about a young bohemian that takes you from black middle-class America to Amsterdam, Berlin and beyond on a journey towards personal and artistic authenticity. "Fresh, exuberant, bracingly inventive, bitingly funny, and full of heart." –*NY Times.* "The freshest musical in town!" –*Wall Street Journal.* "Excellent songs and a vulnerable heart." –*Variety.* [4M, 3W] ISBN: 978-0-8222-2400-6

★ **REASONS TO BE PRETTY by Neil LaBute.** Greg really, truly adores his girlfriend, Steph. Unfortunately, he also thinks she has a few physical imperfections, and when he mentions them, all hell breaks loose. "Tight, tense and emotionally true." –*Time Magazine.* "Lively and compulsively watchable." –*The Record.* [2M, 2W] ISBN: 978-0-8222-2394-8

★ **OPUS by Michael Hollinger.** With only a few days to rehearse a grueling Beethoven masterpiece, a world-class string quartet struggles to prepare their highest-profile performance ever—a televised ceremony at the White House. "Intimate, intense and profoundly moving." –*Time Out.* "Worthy of scores of bravissimos." –*BroadwayWorld.com.* [4M, 1W] ISBN: 978-0-8222-2363-4

★ **BECKY SHAW by Gina Gionfriddo.** When an evening calculated to bring happiness takes a dark turn, crisis and comedy ensue in this wickedly funny play that asks what we owe the people we love and the strangers who land on our doorstep. "As engrossing as it is ferociously funny." –*NY Times.* "Gionfriddo is some kind of genius." –*Variety.* [2M, 3W] ISBN: 978-0-8222-2402-0

★ **KICKING A DEAD HORSE by Sam Shepard.** Hobart Struther's horse has just dropped dead. In an eighty-minute monologue, he discusses what path brought him here in the first place, the fate of his marriage, his career, politics and eventually the nature of the universe. "Deeply instinctual and intuitive." –*NY Times.* "The brilliance is in the infinite reverberations Shepard extracts from his simple metaphor." –*TheaterMania.* [1M, 1W] ISBN: 978-0-8222-2336-8

DRAMATISTS PLAY SERVICE, INC.
440 Park Avenue South, New York, NY 10016 212-683-8960 Fax 212-213-1539
postmaster@dramatists.com www.dramatists.com